Welcome Home

Poems, Musings, and Observations
of Life in the Smoky Mountains

Scott Williamson Thompson

ISBN: 978-1-0878-6913-1

First Edition

DESIGN, PHOTOGRAPHY, AND ART:
Karen E. Reynolds, 'Ker Creatives'

DEDICATION

When a potter pulls a pot, his fingerprints are obvious on the sides of that pot. All my experiences, travels, and all the people I have met, lived with, and come in contact with are obvious on me. We are a large human family, and we influence each other.

I dedicate this book to all of you I have been fortunate to know and who have become part of my family.

Acknowledgments

Presently, I must also dedicate this book to the love of my life, Tish. Somehow we work. She inspires me and challenges me to be as fine and giving a person as she is. She is my energizer bunny, a loving angel of life.

My son, Wes, has given my life fullness. I have been blessed to watch him grow up and become the man he is now. What a gift to have such a son. He gives me much pride and joy, as do my stepdaughters, Kelly and Sarah, who have accepted me into their lives—my cup overflows. I have enjoyed sharing time and experiences with them as they have grown into beautiful women. It was an unexpected bonus to have daughters in my life. All my children have helped me to learn greater definitions of love.

My grandchildren Graham, Adeline, Abel, Ezra, and Kayla have given me blessings way past what I deserve. I am lucky to come from a large family who I thank, and I also thank Tish's family for the gifts of knowing them all. And I have been blessed also with in-laws of our children as our families have all bonded, and love surrounds our grandchildren.

A special thanks to Karen E. Reynolds, who is responsible for this book's fruition. An old friend, a talented musician, and a more talented human being, she has let me lean on her hard work, sacrifices, knowledge, and success to help me put this together. I am forever grateful. Thank you Karen.

Contents

Introduction

In 1970 I missed a fine arts class in college because I was sick. I had to make it up and was sent to the arts department where I was introduced to Dale Bunse. He showed me how to mix some powered clay (earth) with water, how to wedge it, put it on a potter's wheel, and he helped me center it. Then he knocked it off center and told me I had to re-center it myself. It changed my life. Everything became part of the circle of centering, whether my clay, my life, or myself. I learned how to balance myself by balancing the clay. That was when I became bonded with the earth. I had grown up in the city, but it seemed the clay had brought me to the mountains. Now I make my home in the foothills of the Great Smoky Mountains National Park.

When I would center the clay and pull the sides of the pot up, I was also reformed. Time stopped. The clay, my coordination, my breathing, my fingers as the clay passed through them, allowed the world to be sent away. I learned to be where I am, and in the moment. After I pulled pots with the clay, I would glaze them with beautiful colors. Once again, the clay had taught me many things; What is beauty? What is art? I grew up an athlete and knew nothing of art, outside the flow of motion in sports. What colors go together? What definitions have I been taught, and what is real from my eyes? I looked to the clouds and began to see them change colors across the mountains. My eyes were opened to beauty all around that I had ignored, been blind to. A new world appeared before me, sights and colors. As I walked off into the mountains, my nostrils came to life. My skin was awakened as I jumped into the mountain streams and felt a flow of new awareness. Admittedly, I was a terrible English student, but while making pots, I began to write songs and poems. I overflowed. Life was overwhelming. I had to write.

With this book, maybe I can share my joy, taking my words off the walls of my man cave and opening up to you. What else have we each missed by taking for granted our wonderful opportunity to be alive, by making our own definitions of truth instead of being tolerant and open to all that is around us? What truths have we ignored to create our cocooned comfort? Here, I share my own journey. I hope it identifies with yours. We are all children, all of us. We must live and work together to save what truths are important and necessary for our blessed existence. Fight to find truth in life and live. Enjoy. Enjoy.

Thank you for spending a little time with me. If you enjoy our time together, please tell a friend about my book. Thanks.

—Scott

Welcome Home

May your house give you sanctuary and peace.

May it be a refuge for your heart, and a home where you and your loved ones flourish,

where you find the best of who you really are.

May your home show you how great life can be, the better things you want to learn about,
and levels of happiness and companionship unimagined yet.

May your home grow in the glow of the Smoky mist, helping to blend you into the shades of the horizons.

And, like the songs of nature, may your tunes flow full in the waves of the mountain currents.

May the scents of life surround you, so the air of your being is alive with unique tastes.

May you breathe free and see clear all that is around you and drink of it daily.

May you accept all weather and weather all storms.

May you enjoy the seasons as they happen, and in your heart, bonding you to the roots of your life.

And of all of your decorations, may love be the loudest.

Welcome Home

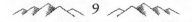

*"I reach now for dreams made,
and dreams yet unknown, but longed for,
waited for."*

Early Spring Sprout

The winter had frozen me.
Finally a warmth surrounds me
seeping through my cracked hull.

The cold I thought would kill me, has opened me
to reach now for dreams made
and dreams yet unknown, but longed for, waited for.

I am a sprout,
my root finding its place in the soil
as equal parts of me reach for the light.

Footprints on the Sunset

I gaze on crystal water and see birds are flying by.
They lead my eyes through mountains as I look up to the sky.
Glimmers and the gurgling bring me back into the flow
as it ripples past reflections I start to sense a tow.

There's a scent of rushing current and the chill upon my face.
A gentle breeze comes to me with such a lovely taste
from up behind the laurel, from the hemlocks and the pines,
through ferns and moss and moisture underneath
the hanging vines.

Warbles, chirps, and whistles from the trees that screech and bend
and whispers of resistance of a steady growing wind,
a rustle in the dry leaves, then the splash by shallow stones
say the circle is so natural that calls my senses home.
A dozen surfing spiders—do they swim or do they run?—
little footprints on the sunset, where the wet and clouds are one.

"Breathe deep.
Taste the call of the wind."

Whisper of Wind

Let the wind whisper.
Inhale the scent as it calls to a sprit within.
Be open and listen and feel all you can.
Breathe deep. Taste the call of the wind.

Birds singing and surfing in currents all around
share music with songs from the creek.
They soothe me, amuse me,
and wisp me inside of the waves of new colors I seek.

Yes, let the wind whisper.
My spirit is gone to a calmness I feel deep within.
I'm off with my freedom. My breath is so full
as I taste of the whisper of wind.

The Unknown Now

Each sparkle of light glimmering off the flowing river
shines on evolving growth, no two moments the same.

As I ride my currents through ever changing scenes,
mountain vistas remind me of past views.
Are my eyes open for what is different?
Do I stay upstream at the pleasant pool or rage
the rapids open to what is new?

I accept the flow and feel its fullness.
I search for new meaning in the undefined present
living neither in yesterday nor tomorrow.
The gifts of life are now. I am molded by my past
and my dreams of the future.
But here is where I am in the unknown now.

*"Motion is the constant,
the brush that paints the sky."*

The Constant

Motion is the constant, the brush that paints the sky.
It designs beneath the water, ripples pictures for my eyes.
It stirs up my emotions and calls when I don't change.
The waves and winds of motion, circle and proclaim.

I sing to steady current by a river near the rocks.
I hear motion in the mountains. I wonder while I watch.
It seems to pull me downhill, toward an ocean rolled with waves.
But I'm walking toward a summit so my eyes can rest and gaze.

Moving wind brings magic scents to imprint me while I'm here.
They remind me of this calmness and release me of my fear
'til the rain and storms rage with life again and demand
my deep respect.
Then a calmness always follows as the rhythm here is set.

Motion is the constant, the brush that paints the sky.
It travels in a circle and stays part of our lives.

*"I've tried to let my mind live wild
and free out on the range."*

Hills of Echoes

I still live in hills of echoes of years I've lived before.

Did I learn from my own common sense or was it more the lore?

I've tried to keep the range wide open and think before the fence,

respectful watching tolerance of acres of abyss.

So many great realities of uncontrolled terrain!

I've tried to let my mind live wild and free out on the range.

Yet I still live in hills of echoes of years I've lived before

that thunder all around me as I ride the range for more.

Dandelion

I'm like a dandelion
blown by the wind, lifted here and there, wherever.

I envy the vine creeping, held to the ground.
But I enjoy my fleeting view, the distance I travel,
the unknowns that happen.

I also long for the foundation of the vine.
Soon I will claim my soil.

But now I fly.

*"My nostrils are full
with the anticipation of rain."*

Hot Spring Rain

My nostrils are full with the anticipation of rain.
It's aroma mixes with all the life around to present
a buffet of smells and tastes.

The humidity, it's other messenger, coats everything
I touch and wets my shirt and forehead.
My skin sticks to my pants as the dust to my arms.

Then comes the first hard rain since the flowers
have blossomed. Rain carries trails of pollen downstream.

The mountains hide behind the rain, mist, and clouds.
I wait for the sun to burn a path to my eyes.

Snug in the Mountains

Stay safe in the shade of the mountains that holds you so snug in
it's sights
of currents of colors that change through the day as they play
with the layers of light.
And breathe of the gift of the mist here that brings you the presents
of scents
of balsam, and hemlocks, and hardwoods, and pines that the
shade, sun, and rivers accent.
Hear wind through the trees as the birds sing. Life hides in the
blankets of leaves.
The quiet is full of the whispers of life that surround you in one
gentle breeze.
The loud river's roar is so peaceful. Drowns out the confusion
you feel.
It captures your spirit and takes you down stream and reminds
you in life what is real.
Now walk that journey inside you alive in the visions you see.
Relax in your currents. Sway like the trees.
So snug in the mountains, be free.

*"No matter where I go,
the light is always there."*

Constant Light

Last bursts of light make their way across the horizon
and around me,
engulfing me in the changing colors as they battle
to furnish the last rays of the day
and welcome a coming of a dark sky full of stars
and new colors.

I enjoy this circle.
I watch the moon rise, positioning itself to reflect
the sun into long trails of lapping light
on an unending mountain lake; leading back to me,
a path to the sun.
No matter where I go,
the light is always there.

I Smell the Hickory

I smell the hickory burning in the fireplace.
I taste the colors dancing on the sky.
I feel the mountain changing all its colors as the wind blows.
I'm melted on the path the river goes.

My ears can see the mouths of young birds feeding.
My sides are bent as tops of trees be blown.
My eyes can taste the mist upon the hillside changing colors.
My wings are stretched, I'm about to fly.
My eyes searched long but now my mind can whistle.
My toes can touch the moss upon the ground.
My face can sense the weather and my nose can taste the dawn.
And my ears can hear the pleasures of the day.

Cause I'm home back here in the country.
Got no one to tell me what to do.
Got no noise or rapid locomotion.
Chickens give me eggs. Squirrels bring me news.

*"The energy of this day grows as the sun sets,
beginning the final burning of this light
that gives birth to a new evening."*

Sunset

A fire from the sun is alive in these low clouds
and reflects down on the hills,
the last celebrations of today, painting
the trees that are changing colors in the mountain haze.

The humidity is gone and a cool taste of fresh
and new accents the early dusk.
The delicious breeze is clean,
taking these clouds away.

The energy of this day grows as the sun sets,
beginning the final burning of this light
that gives birth to a new evening.

*"Our cycle is our cycle
as we bake in the sun."*

Crystals on the Ground

Mist rises off the water on a cold night to the tune
of the mountain stream.
Small clouds are lamp shades to the moon, brightening the sky.

The frost burned leaves hanging to dry, are wet in the mist
of night, iced by early morning,
dried by the afternoon, waiting for the wind or the morning
coat of white.

Our cycle is our cycle as we bake in the sun.
The evening mist again rises off the motions of moisture,
coating us with life as we accept the chill of dusk, the ice of night.

The leaves and grasses shine in the moonlight,
crystals on the ground.

Breathe My Breath from Momma

The breathing of our planet in the early morning winds
is whispered in the treetops in the motion of the limbs.

And the winds of waving waters and ever changing skies
let me look at Momma, squarely in the eyes.

I bask daily in her beauty, in all the tunes she sings.
I swim in veins of water, alive in all she brings.

The bare trees on the mountains look like lungs out in the air.
I think that Momma's breathing when I feel her in my hair.

She's here upon the table. I'm wrapped within her coat.
I breathe my breath from Momma and feel her loving strokes.

*"See the miracle of a shooting star
in December."*

Cold Winter Night

Turn off the lights, this cold winter night!
Our fears that we hide from with man-made lights
have made our land so bright, we miss the real sights.
Go sit by the water. Lie down in a field.
Take a walk by the woods where the sky is revealed.

Be away from our kingdom of man-made lights.
Do you a favor and be there at night.
Open your eyes with your ears and your nose.
Taste of the touch of the night you bestow.
Listen and smell and look and feel
and see the infinity of light that is real.

In the magic of this dark so alive from the night
see that light that can guide us away from the light.
See the miracle of a shooting star in December.

"I inhale this day and its beauty."

January Rain

This January rain is a steady drizzle,
occasionally more, for a time.
Then constant mist lights the leaves with reflections off
the frozen drops, lengthening with time and cold.
The thickness of the ice surrounds stems, and needles,
and bushes, and grass.
Shiny sparkles are clear pictures of an arctic moment
that steal my attention.

There's a splash, then a slip or a slide. I look all around
at a moment encased in ice.
Grabbing for balance, there's a chill on my face.
Frost from my breath returns the cool wet clean
taste of life, warmed, to the air.
I inhale this day and its beauty.

Middle of February up in the Smokies

The fall leaves are wrapped tight on the forest floor
cooking the spring
buds that are snaking their way out to the light.

The wind talks through the branches nearby,
then dances with the tree tops.
The sun explodes from behind the hurried cloud.

Deer tracks are on the trail that I'm walking.
Even the squirrels and birds can't move quietly
through these layered leaves.

Acorns sprout next to the snow.
A cloud slams the door shut on the sun
and an instant chill surrounds me.

"It's not always what we take away, sometimes, it's what we bring."

Where the Bears Walked

This is where the bears walked, this place I park my car,
underneath a streetlight where the wolves howled at the stars.

The paths where all the deer ran are covered up with tar and
numbers on the front curb tell us who we are.
Filter all our water. We can't drink from the streams.
You see, we've done it our way to fit with all our dreams.
Just what is it we are searching for and what is it we've seen?
There's hormones in the milk we drink and we skim off
all the cream.

Let's see the definitions of how we live our lives.
There are very simple truths around that we should realize.
Plant a tree for Ruthie so she can have a swing.
Leave some land for wildlife and other living things.
Protect some ground for solitude to swim and laugh and sing.
It's not always what we take away. Sometimes, it's what we bring.

This is where the bears walked, this place I park my car,
underneath a streetlight where the wolves howled at the stars.

I'm Older and I'm Younger

I'm older than this morning. I'm younger than tonight.
It depends on how you measure with the sunshine and the light.
I'm older than spring flowers. I'm younger than these trees.
We've all been here a long time though, all cycles of a seed.

I'm young with what I've learned today held in a weathered net.
I'm newer now than I was before the older that I get.
Moments, habits, seasons, lives have been and yet will be.
Perceptions keep on changing like the sky for us to see.

Years go by despite myself no matter what I do.
But I don't feel much older with this so-called senior view.
Another child is born today. Another old man dies.
But I'll just keep on living the way I see things through my eyes.

I'm older than this morning. I'm younger than tonight.
It depends on how you measure with the sunshine and the light.

"The faces, the actions, the ticks of time,
forgot the clock and never left."

Some Memories

Some memories of my past are vivid in my present,
as real and clear as their creations, lives ago.
Time and weather try to put those moments far away
and cloud my view.

But those parts of me that made me are here,
now, exciting, full and bright in my eyes, ears, and being.

The faces, the actions, the ticks of time,
forgot the clock and never left,
alive today, timeless... timeless and ageless and infinite,
new as the spirit that lives in this aging temple.

Where I'll Rest

When you take my ashes, to put me in that jar,
walk up to the mountains. Go way up there, past far.
Hike up to the highest bald where you lean into the wind.
Take a whiff of wildness, then forgive me of my sins.

Leave a dash of me behind. That's where I always was
and where I'll always wanna be when the day light turns to dusk.
Then head down to that mountain stream where it's deep enough
     to dip.
Take off all your worldly goods and give yourself a sit.

Now smile once for the gleam you saw, that was always in my eyes
and know that I am with you in the colors in the sky.
Look around you reverently at the beauty always there
and know that I am part of you in the vision that we share.
Please spread me round the mountain mist where I always felt at
     home.
I'll be there if you want me, if you ever feel alone.